COOL SCIENCE

SCIENCE BEATS CRIME

John Perritano

mc **Marshall Cavendish**
Benchmark

New York

This edition first published in 2011 in the United States
by Marshall Cavendish Benchmark.

Marshall Cavendish Benchmark
99 White Plains Road
Tarrytown, NY 10591
www.marshallcavendish.us

Published by Marshall Cavendish Benchmark
An imprint of Marshall Cavendish Corporation

Other Marshall Cavendish Offices:
Marshall Cavendish International (Asia) Private Limited, 1 New Industrial Road, Singapore 536196 • Marshall Cavendish
International (Thailand) Co Ltd. 253 Asoke, 12th Flr, Sukhumvit 21 Road, Klongtoey Nua, Wattana, Bangkok 10110, Thailand •
Marshall Cavendish (Malaysia) Sdn Bhd, Times Subang, Lot 46, Subang Hi-Tech Industrial Park, Batu Tiga, 40000 Shah Alam,
Selangor Darul Ehsan, Malaysia

Marshall Cavendish is a trademark of Times Publishing Limited

Library of Congress Cataloging-in-Publication Data
Perritano, John.
Science beats crime / John Perritano.
p. cm. – (Cool science)
Includes index.
ISBN 978-1-60870-078-3
1. Forensic sciences–Juvenile literature. 2. Criminal
investigation–Juvenile literature. I. Title.
HV8073.8.P47 2011
363.25–dc22
2009053774

Created by Q2AMedia
Series Editor: Bonnie Dobkin
Art Director: Harleen Mehta
Client Service Manager: Santosh Vasudevan
Project Manager: Kumar Kunal
Line Artist: Vinay Kumar
Coloring Artist: Subhash Vohra
Photo research: Ekta Sharma, Rajeev Parmar
Designer: Cheena Yadav

The photographs in this book are used by permission and through the courtesy of:

Cover: Timothy R. Nichols/Shutterstock; Scott Rothstein/Shutterstock; Dario Sabljak/Shutterstock; Katrina Brown/Shutterstock
Half title: Timothy R. Nichols/Shutterstock; Myotis/Shutterstock

4: Outlook/Corbis Sygma; 5: FogStock LLC/Photolibrary; 7: Rex Features; 8: Dusan Po/Shutterstock; 9: Peter Kim/Istockphoto;
10: Ho/AP Photo; 11: AP Photo; 12: Benjamin Albiach Galan/Shutterstock; 13: Peter Dazeley/Getty Images; 14: Mike Rieger/FEMA
News Photo; 16l: AP Photo; 16r: San Quentin State Prison; 17: Justin Sullivan/Stringer/Getty Images; 18: Natalie Petrovsky;
19: Ron Cardy/Rex Features; 20t: Andrew Unangst/Shutterstock; 20b: Michael Williams/Getty Images; 22: Irene Wairimu/AFP;
23: Forensic Microscopes; 24t: Timothy R. Nichols/Shutterstock, 24b Jubal Harshaw/Shutterstock; 25: Steger Volker/Peter Arnold
Images/Photolibrary; 26t: Anthony Bolante/Reuters, 26bl: Ho Old/Reuters, 26br: Ho Old/Reuters; 27: Cheryl Hatch/AP Photo;
28: John Sommers II/Reuters; 29: John Sommers II/Reuters; 30: Paul Wilkinson/Istockphoto; 31: Capital Pictures; 32: Newspix/
Rex Features; 33: Michael Luckett/Fotolia; 34: Zora/Fotolia; 35: Phil Ball/Rex Features; 36: Drainhook/Flickr; 37l: Sinclair
Stammers/Science Photo Library; 37r: Michigan State University; 38: Mary Evans Picture Library/Photolibrary; 39: Evan Agostini/
Getty Images; 40: Timothy Hughes Rare & Early Newspapers; 41: AP Photo; 42: David Longstreet/AP Photo;
43: Karen Kasmauski/Science Faction/Corbis; 45l: Istockphoto, 45r: Liang Zhang/Istockphoto

Q2AMedia Art Bank: 6, 21

Printed in Malaysia (T)

1 3 5 6 4 2

CONTENTS

SCENE OF THE CRIME

It begins with a frantic 911 call. A man out walking his dog has spotted a woman's body lying just outside the front door of a house.

Police arrive and put yellow crime scene tape around the area to keep people away. Special crime scene investigators soon pull up. They look for evidence—clues as to what might have happened and who might be responsible for the murder. They notice a trail of blood leading away from the body.

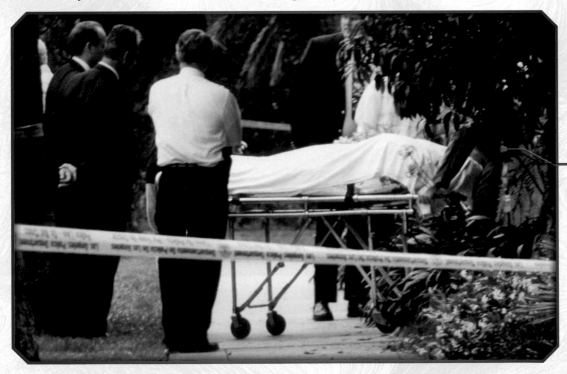

A body is removed from the scene of a murder.

Police suspect the murderer was injured during the attack and bled while fleeing the scene. Investigators carefully place the evidence in special bags and whisk it off to the police laboratory. As lab technicians analyze the blood, detectives identify a suspect—the woman's estranged husband.

At the husband's apartment complex, investigators find spots of blood on the steering wheel of his car. The blood matches that of the victim. The scientists also determine that the blood taken from the crime scene matches the suspect's blood. Using this and other evidence, police make an arrest.

Real-World Drama

Terrible crimes like this occur every day. And every day, police use forensic science, the study of crime scene evidence, to find leads, track down criminals, and provide evidence.

In criminal courts, prosecutors try to convict those charged with a crime. Sometimes, prosecutors rely on eyewitness testimony, or statements made by people who see something related to a crime. Eyewitnesses are often unreliable, however. They can be confused about details of the crime. Sometimes they change their minds about what they saw, or withhold part of the truth.

A better way to win a conviction is to use forensic evidence. If handled properly, forensic evidence never lies and never gets confused. It can be the surest way to catch a criminal.

During a trial, an attorney presents forensic evidence to help support his case.

CRIME BUSTERS

Forensic science has been around for hundreds of years. In 1807, the University of Edinburgh in Scotland formed one of the first schools for the study of forensics.

Then, in the late 1800s, the exploits of a fictional detective named Sherlock Holmes inspired real-life French **criminologist** Edmond Locard to build the first crime laboratory in Lyon, France. Locard used the lab to study crime scene evidence. Known as the father of forensic science, Locard wrote that criminals always leave tiny clues, such as clothing fibers, behind at the crime scene.

Sherlock Holmes, Sir Arthur Conan Doyle's famous fictional detective, solved crimes using observation and logic. The smallest bits of evidence provided him with a wealth of information.

Forensic Wizards

Today, forensic science is as varied as the crimes police try to solve. At the head of these investigations are crime scene investigators, or CSIs. They painstakingly collect evidence at the crime scene. Forensic scientists then examine that evidence.

There are many types of forensic scientists. One group includes **toxicologists**, experts who look for the presence of drugs, alcohol, and other substances in the body's tissues and blood. **Medical examiners** are forensic scientists who perform **autopsies** to determine the time and cause of death.

Some forensic scientists study blood splatters. Others, such as forensic **entomologists**, search for clues by looking at the insects found on, near, or in a corpse. Ballistics experts study guns and the path bullets take when fired. Forensic **anthropologists** use the remains of skeletons to figure out how a person died and what they might have looked like when they were alive.

Forensic science is fascinating, and it is becoming more sophisticated every day.

CSIs carefully collect evidence from a crime scene where a body was found. They wear gloves, special suits, and shoe covers to make sure the evidence isn't contaminated.

POINTING THE FINGER

Look at the tips of your fingers. Do you see a series of lines, ridges, loops, and curves? These are your fingerprints. Each has its own pattern, and no two are the same.

In 1880, Scottish physician Henry Faulds suggested for the first time that police could use fingerprints to identify criminals. Fingerprints soon became one of the most important types of evidence an investigator could collect. When fingerprints are found at a crime scene, they prove that a certain person was there at some point.

There are three basic fingerprint patterns: the loop, the whorl, and the arch.

A person can leave fingerprints on doorknobs, windowpanes, even drinking glasses. How are fingerprints formed? Sweat glands lie just beneath the skin of our hands and fingers. These sweat glands ooze oils through tiny holes known as pores. The oil mixes with perspiration. When a person touches a surface, the mixture creates an image of the finger on that surface.

Dust and Lift

There are two categories of fingerprints: *patent* prints, which can easily be seen, and *latent* prints, which are hidden.

Some CSIs use a special powder and brush to reveal fingerprints. The dust sticks to the oil left by the criminal's fingers. Investigators may also use lasers—narrow beams of high-intensity lights—to find prints. At other times, they'll use superglue! The fumes from the glue react with the skin oil to make the prints visible.

Once a CSI finds a print, he or she uses a special tape to lift it from the surface. The tape is carefully placed on a card or piece of paper and sent to a forensic lab for analysis. The print is then sent to a lab for analysis.

A technician dusts for fingerprints.

Tools of the Trade

The Integrated Automated Fingerprint Identification System

When police collect someone's fingerprints, they send those prints to a national computer database run by the Federal Bureau of Investigation (FBI). The Integrated Automated Fingerprint Identification System has fingerprints on file for more than 55 million criminals. Local police departments can tap into the database and identify fingerprints within minutes.

Polly Klaas

Polly Hannah Klaas was just like any other twelve-year-old girl. She enjoyed going to the movies. She loved school. She enjoyed spending time with her friends.

When: October 1, 1993
Where: Petaluma, California
Crime: Murder
Suspect: Richard Allen Davis
Evidence: Palm print

CASE CLOSED

Kidnapped

On October 1, 1993, Polly and two friends were having a pajama party. Without warning, a stranger crawled into Polly's house through an open window. He held a knife. The intruder tied up all the girls. He put pillow cases over their heads. He then dragged Polly off.

The kidnapping stunned the nation. The press called Polly "America's Child." Television news shows, including *America's Most Wanted*, featured the kidnapping in the hopes of finding Polly.

This 1993 photo of Polly Klaas became known throughout the country.

A Palm Print

A couple of months later, police arrested Richard Allen Davis. Davis fit the description Polly's friends gave of the kidnapper. Police were also able to connect a palm print on the bed to Davis. Police used a special light and powder to find the invisible print on the bed railing.

Davis confessed to the crime. He then led police to where he had hidden Polly's body. A jury found Davis guilty of murder. He is on California's death row, waiting to be executed.

Richard Davis, as he appeared in court on an unrelated drunk driving charge in 1993.

THE INCREDIBLE WORLD OF DNA

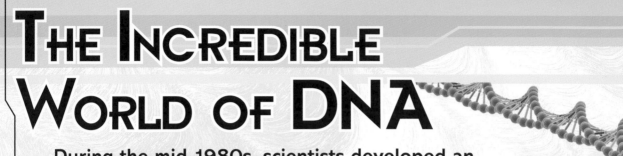

During the mid-1980s, scientists developed an almost surefire way to catch criminals, identify victims, free prisoners, and solve old mysteries. They called the method DNA profiling.

DNA is short for *deoxyribonucleic acid*. DNA is a spiral-shaped molecule found in the body's cells. It contains a person's genes, which determine characteristics such as eye and hair color.

Certain parts of DNA are unique to each individual. Scientists have found several ways to locate and analyze these one-of-kind genetic fingerprints. The result is known as a DNA profile. Police can create a DNA profile by removing DNA from sweat, blood, **saliva**, and hair left at the crime scene. They then compare that evidence to DNA taken from a suspect or victim.

The information in DNA is stored as a code made up of four chemical bases: adenine, guanine, cytosine, and thymine.

Wrongly Convicted

Before scientists developed DNA profiling, many individuals were convicted of crimes they never committed. Some spent years, even decades, waiting for evidence that would clear them. Now, scientists can use DNA profiling to prevent innocent people from being thrown in jail. Profiling can also be used to free people who are already there.

Such was the case with twenty-two-year-old Bill Dillon. In 1981, a Florida jury convicted Dillon of murder. The jury's decision was based on the testimony of John Preston. Preston claimed his scent-tracking dog tied Dillon to the killer's bloody yellow T-shirt.

Years later, authorities discovered that Preston was a fraud. Finally, in 2007, scientists examined the blood on the T-shirt. One DNA profile matched that of the victim. The DNA of two unknown individuals was also found on the T-shirt. But there was no DNA on the shirt linking Dillon to the crime! Dillon left prison after spending twenty-seven years behind bars.

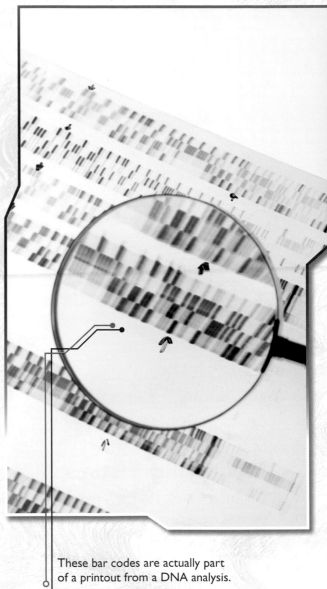

These bar codes are actually part of a printout from a DNA analysis.

Inside Knowledge

In 1988, British prosecutors used DNA for the first time to identify Colin Pitchfork as the murderer of two young girls. That same year, prosecutors in the United States used DNA to convict Tommy Lee Andrews for assaulting several people in Orlando, Florida. In both cases, DNA found in samples taken from the victims were matched to the suspects.

Identifying Victims

Scientists also use DNA to identify victims of crimes or disasters. Many times, police will find a badly **decomposed** body days, months, and even years after death. Scientists can often track down who that person was by extracting DNA from the body or bones and comparing it to DNA taken from family members.

That's exactly what happened when terrorists flew two planes into the World Trade Center in New York City on September 11, 2001. Scientists used DNA to determine the identity of 1,597 of the 2,789 World Trade Center victims.

Rescue workers at the World Trade Center were trained not to overlook anything they found. Even the tiniest piece of clothing or bit of bone could provide enough DNA for scientists to identify a victim.

Mysteries Solved . . . Sometimes

The DNA of any living thing will begin to break down after the organism's death. Exposure to moisture, sunlight, and air will speed the process. Still, DNA samples can be taken from very old remains. (DNA has even been extracted from Egyptian mummies!) That means DNA profiling can be used to shed new light on old cases. Investigators now use this tool to look back at *cold* cases—cases that no one could solve. The results can be both surprising and disturbing.

THE STRANGE CASE OF HAWLEY CRIPPEN

Hawley Crippen was a quiet, well-mannered English doctor. In January 1910, his wife Cora suddenly disappeared. Crippen told people that she had died while visiting relatives in the United States.

Cora's friends became suspicious and called police. The doctor now said that Cora had run off with another man. Police searched his home. They found many body parts under the house. Eventually, Crippen was hanged for his wife's murder. Before he died, Crippen wrote, "I am innocent and some day evidence will be found to prove it."

That day arrived nearly one hundred years later. Modern-day researchers compared Cora Crippen's DNA, found on a microscopic slide used in the case, to the DNA of her surviving relatives. The DNA from the body under the house did not match the DNA from Cora's relatives. So whose body parts were under the house? No one knows for sure.

Laci Peterson

When: December 24, 2002

Where: Modesto, California

Crime: Murder

Suspect: Scott Peterson

Evidence: DNA

CASE CLOSED

Laci and Scott Peterson seemed to have the perfect marriage. That image was shattered on December 24, 2002, when Laci Peterson vanished from their home in Modesto, California. The twenty-seven-year-old was eight months pregnant. Scott Peterson called police later that day to report her missing. He said he had been on his boat, fishing in the San Francisco Bay, when she vanished.

It turned out, though, that Scott had a girlfriend who had known nothing of Laci. She had met Scott two weeks before Laci disappeared. When news about Scott and Laci hit the media, the girlfriend grew suspicious and went to the police.

Laci Peterson, not long before she disappeared.

SAN QUENTIN STATE PRISON
PETERSON, S.
V-72100

Scott Peterson's mug shot.

Bodies in the Bay

DNA provided a break in the case when a **fetus** washed up on the shore of San Francisco Bay on April 13, 2003. The next day, a woman walking her dog found the remains of a woman. The area was near where Peterson said he was fishing the day Laci disappeared. Scientists used DNA to identify the remains as those of Laci and her unborn child.

Police now suspected that Peterson had killed his wife and tossed her body from the boat into the bay. When they searched his boat, they found two strands of human hair on a pair of needle-nose pliers. Police hoped the hair on the pliers belonged to Laci, who witnesses had said never went on the boat.

Scientists tested the hair for DNA. They ran into problems. They could not remove *nuclear DNA* from the hair. A person's nuclear DNA is inherited from both parents. It can positively identify a person.

Instead, scientists had to test for *mitochondrial DNA*, which comes only from the mother. This could only be used to show a strong likelihood that the hair belonged to Laci. Still, the jury believed the DNA, as well as other evidence. Scott Peterson was convicted of Laci's murder.

17

Anastasia, the Missing Duchess

It was one of the great mysteries of the twentieth century. Had Anastasia, the youngest daughter of Czar Nicholas II of Russia, been murdered along with the rest of the royal family during the Russian Revolution? Or had she and her younger brother, Alexei, escaped the slaughter? Now, thanks to forensic science, the mystery has been solved.

When: July 17, 1918

Where: Yekaterinburg, Russia

Crime: Murder

Suspect: Russian revolutionaries

Evidence: DNA

CASE CLOSED

The story of Anastasia began on July 17, 1918. That's when revolutionaries shot and stabbed Czar Nicholas and the rest of the Romanov family. The bodies, however, were never located.

This photo shows Czar Nicholas, Czarina Alexandra, and their children. Anastasia is on the far right of the picture.

These remains, belonging to Czar Nicholas and members of his family, were found in a grave near Yekaterinburg, Russia.

People kept hoping that Anastasia had survived. In fact, over the years, several people claimed they were Anastasia, including a woman named Anna Anderson. Hopes that Anastasia had escaped her family's fate were bolstered in 1991. That's when researchers found a grave containing Nicholas, his wife, Alexandra, and other members of the Romanov family. Missing from the grave were the remains of Anastasia and Alexei.

The grave's discovery paved the way for DNA testing. In 1994, scientists analyzed DNA taken from a lock of Anna Anderson's hair. Anderson had died in 1984. Scientists found that Anderson's DNA did not match DNA taken from the czar and his wife.

The mystery continued. Then researchers discovered a second grave in 2007. Inside that grave were the bones of two children. Scientists analyzed DNA from the second grave and compared it to the DNA taken from the czar and his wife. The DNA matched. The bones in the second grave were those of Anastasia and Alexei.

THE SCIENCE OF BALLISTICS

Guns are the weapon of choice for most criminals. That's why a whole branch of forensic science is dedicated to studying them: ballistics.

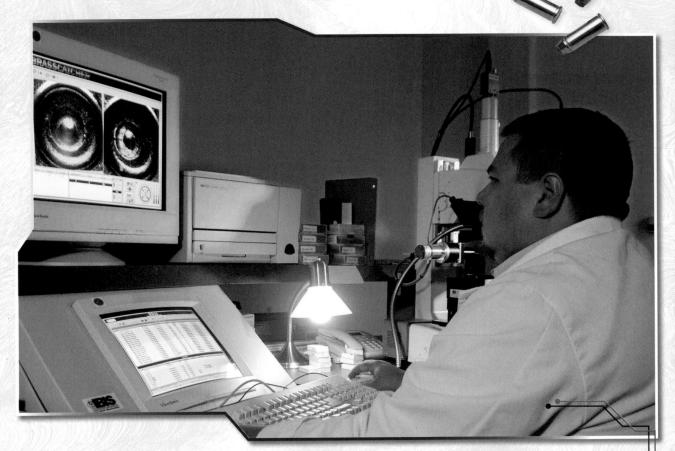

In 1902, Oliver Wendell Holmes proved for the first time in a United States courtroom that a specific gun had been used as a murder weapon. Holmes had a gunsmith test fire the gun into a wad of cotton. He then compared the marks on the crime scene bullet to the marks on the test-fired bullet. They were a perfect match.

A forensic scientist examines shell casings with the aid of a computer that links him to crime labs around the country.

The science of forensic ballistics grew from that point on. Experts in this area examine both the guns and the ammunition used in crimes. Sometimes the goal is simply to determine what weapon was used. At other times, the aim is to match a bullet with a specific gun.

Ballistic Fingerprints

How does ballistics work? Guns leave "fingerprints," just like humans do. Inside a gun barrel are grooves. These grooves cause a bullet to spin. Spinning makes the flight of the bullet more accurate. As a bullet speeds through the gun, the grooves leave telltale marks on the bullet. By comparing these marks, ballistics experts can tell whether a specific gun fired a specific bullet.

Investigators can also use casings found at the scene of the crime. Casings house the bullet and the gunpowder that propel the bullet through the gun barrel. Ballistics experts can match the marks on a casing to a specific type of gun.

Experts used ballistics to investigate the shooting of President John F. Kennedy and Governor John Connally. The evidence indicated that more than one gunman was involved.

INSIDE KNOWLEDGE

The Path of a Bullet

A bullet's *trajectory*, or path, is another important clue for investigators. Studying the path of one bullet helped establish a case for multiple gunmen in the assassination of President John F. Kennedy on November 22, 1963.

The official government report claimed that the wounds suffered by Kennedy and Governor John Connally, who was sitting in front of him in a motorcade, were made by one bullet. But experts continued to study the bullet's trajectory, as well as the entrance and exit wounds. Soon many people began to believe that one bullet could not have traveled the way the original report said. The debate continued for years. Finally, in 2007, researchers at Texas A&M University used state-of-the-art ballistics to provide strong evidence against the lone gunman theory.

- - - - bullet trajectory
● entrance and exit wounds

Danny Vine, Della Thornton

When: January 16, 1991
Where: Camden, Tennessee
Crime: Murder
Suspects: Gary, Robert, and Jerry Lee Bruce; David Riales
Evidence: Ballistics

CASE CLOSED

← The remains of Danny Vine and Della Thornton were so badly burned they were little more than powder.

For years, Danny Vine had made a living diving and selling freshwater mussels near Camden, Tennessee. Little did he know that his work would lead to his death.

On January 16, 1991, Danny Vine's trailer was set ablaze. Thousands of dollars worth of mussels were stolen. Police found the charred skeletal remains of two victims. The fire was so intense that their bones almost turned to powder.

Police took the remains to the crime lab. They victims were identified as Danny Vine and his fiancée, Della Thornton. Scientists X-rayed the skulls. The X rays revealed bullet fragments. Police had also found a bullet casing at the scene. The bullet came from a .38 caliber gun.

As police investigated the murders, they got a break in the case. Someone had bought a truckload of mussels that were dry instead of wet, as mussels should be. Thinking there was something wrong with the mussels, the man called police.

When police asked the man for a receipt, they saw a name they knew too well: Bruce. Police knew the Bruce brothers. Jerry Lee, Gary, and Robert were bad news. At different times, they'd been arrested for robbery, drunk driving, and drugs. Police surmised the mussels the man had bought were the ones stolen from Vine.

A second break in the case came when a woman, a friend of Gary's, overheard a conversation about Gary getting rid of a handgun. Gary had once shown her the gun, and had even shot a round into a tree. The woman told police and showed them the tree Gary had shot into. Police removed the bullet from the tree and compared it to the bullets they had taken from the crime scene. The bullets matched the ones pulled from the skulls of the victims. This discovery led to other evidence that allowed a jury to convict the Bruce brothers and their friend David Riales of murder. All are spending the rest of their lives in jail.

eyepiece

TOOLS OF THE TRADE

Comparison Microscope
In the late 1920s, the science of ballistics got a huge boost when Dr. Calvin Goddard and his partner, Philip Gravelle, adapted the comparison microscope to aid in the study of firearms. For the first time, experts could easily compare the markings on two different bullets.

bullets

WITHOUT A TRACE

Edmond Locard, the father of forensics, said that a criminal always leaves something behind. That something is called trace evidence.

Trace evidence is a very small piece of evidence left at a crime scene. It may come in many forms, including hair, clothing fibers, bloodstains, paint, and pieces of glass.

When a CSI enters a crime scene, he or she must first decide on likely places to find trace evidence. Rough surfaces, such as an upholstered sofa or rug, are good places to find trace evidence. Sharp objects, such as a broken window, may collect fibers from a criminal's torn clothing.

Carpet fibers like these, found at a crime scene, could match the carpet in a suspect's house. This would help connect that person to the crime.

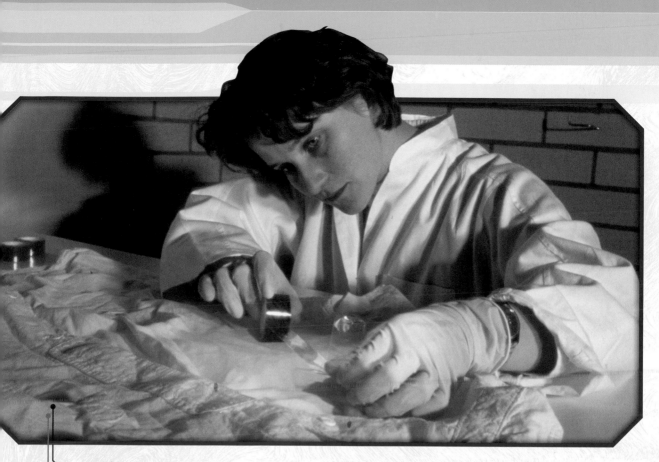

A technician uses special tape to lift fiber evidence from an article of clothing.

Hairs and Fibers

A single strand of hair can provide a lot of information. Forensic scientists can determine whether the hair came from a human or an animal. They can tell the race of a person and what part of the body the hair came from. They can also figure out whether that person had a disease or used specific drugs.

Like hair, traces of fibers from clothes, carpets, and other **textiles** can be critical in solving cases. Small pieces of thread or fibers can link a person directly to a crime scene. Suspects might tear their clothes on a jutting nail, or leave traces of fibers on their victims.

TOOLS OF THE TRADE

Isotopic Hair Analysis

A new crime-fighting technique is being used to help police track the previous movements of unidentified murder victims or suspects. Scientists can now figure out where a person lived by looking for the differences in hydrogen and oxygen **isotopes** in hair samples.

Here's how the process works. The levels of hydrogen and oxygen isotopes in water vary from region to region. So hydrogen and oxygen isotopes found in hair can tell police where someone lived weeks or even years ago. The Salt Lake City Sheriff's Department in Utah is already using the process to identify a murder victim whose remains were found in 2000.

Gary Ridgway, a.k.a. The Green River Killer

When: 1980s
Where: Washington State
Crime: Murder
Suspect: Gary Ridgway
Evidence: Paint particles

CASE CLOSED

On August 15, 1982, Robert Ainsworth was rafting down the Green River near Seattle, Washington, when he spied something in the water. As he got closer, Ainsworth realized to his horror that it was the corpse of a woman. He then spotted another floating body. When police arrived, they made another gruesome discovery— a third corpse.

Police realized a serial killer was on the loose. They called him "The Green River Killer."

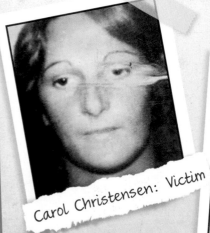

Carol Christensen: Victim

Marcia F. Chapman: Victim

↑ Although Gary Ridgway was a suspect in the murders for years, police lacked the evidence to arrest him.

Gary Ridgway, a factory worker, first became a suspect in 1983, when he was arrested after the disappearance of a woman named Marie Malvar. At the time, though, police didn't have enough evidence to convict him for the Green River killings. Four years later, police arrested Ridgway again on charges not related to the murders. By this time, Ridgway had become the chief suspect in the killings. Still, the evidence wasn't strong enough.

Finally, in 2001, police were able to use DNA profiling to tie Ridgway to some of the victims. In addition, police found microscopic paint particles on several of the bodies. Those paint particles matched the type of truck paint Ridgway used at Kenworth Truck Company, where he had worked for thirty-two years.

In 2003, Ridgway pleaded guilty to forty-eight murders. He escaped execution only by agreeing to help police locate the remains of other victims.

Chain of Custody

When a CSI finds trace evidence at the scene of the crime, he or she must collect and label it correctly and take it to the police station. At the station, police log the evidence and send it to the lab for analysis. This process is called the *chain of custody*. If any step of the chain is missed, defense attorneys can claim the evidence may have been tampered with. Then it can't be used at the time of trial.

Detectives search for evidence in the backyard of Ridgway's home.

THE BODY FARM

At the University of Tennessee's Anthropological Research Facility, the dead have a lot to say. The facility is known as the Body Farm.

There are no cows or sheep on this farm. Instead, there are dozens of dead humans. Scientists at the Body Farm study how human remains decompose over time.

The scientists place actual bodies in different situations. Some are placed in shallow graves or buried in mud. Others are put in parked cars baking in the hot Tennessee sun. Some bodies are burned. Others are submerged in water. A few lack arms and legs. Insects feed on rotting flesh.

Researcher's observe each body's decomposition process and keep careful records. Notes are taken on the sequence of events and the speed with which they occur. Afterward, the bones are used for research and teaching.

Look closely and you can see one of the dead bodies used to provide information at the Body Farm. Also notice the snow in the background. The temperature is one of the details noted by researchers.

Farmer Bill

Dr. Bill Bass became head of the anthropology department at the University of Tennessee in 1971. He was often consulted by police on cases involving decomposing human remains.

Bass wanted to learn more about the subject, so in 1981 he created the Body Farm facility on a 2.5 acre (1 hectare) wooded plot behind the university. He wanted to study the way the human body decays. His research has helped many forensic scientists identify murder victims, figure out time frames, and solve crimes.

Bodies aren't the only things talking at the Body Farm. As a body slowly rots, it oozes chemicals and minerals into the surrounding soil. By studying that dirt, scientists can figure out how long the body has been there. Such experiments help police figure out whether someone was killed at a certain location or somewhere else.

People donate their bodies to the Body Farm. There's a list of 1,600 people who would like to give their bodies to the facility when they die.

Dr. Bill Bass has written both fiction and nonfiction books based on his experiences at the Body Farm.

TRUE BLOOD

Blood can answer a number of important questions about a crime. It can even help identify a murderer.

Blood must be collected carefully. If it is still wet, the CSI uses a gauze pad or a clean cotton cloth to collect it. The blood is allowed to dry. The sample is then placed inside an evidence bag and stored in a freezer or refrigerator. If dried blood is found on an article of clothing, the CSI puts the clothing in a brown paper bag or box. If blood is found on a hard surface, the CSI collects the sample by scraping it off with a clean knife.

The blood is sent to the lab for analysis. DNA can be extracted from it and used for identification. Scientists can also match the blood to a victim or suspect by determining blood type. They do this by testing the blood's red cells for two antigens, or proteins. Those antigens are known as type A and type B.

The bloodstains at this crime scene will provide valuable forensic evidence.

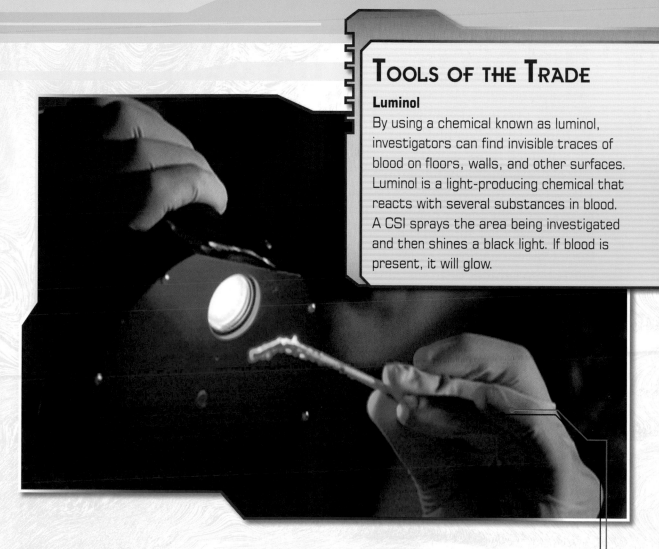

Luminol

By using a chemical known as luminol, investigators can find invisible traces of blood on floors, walls, and other surfaces. Luminol is a light-producing chemical that reacts with several substances in blood. A CSI sprays the area being investigated and then shines a black light. If blood is present, it will glow.

An investigator looks for blood on an object that has been treated with luminol.

Blood Splatters

Blood splatter experts can look at the pattern of blood at a scene and piece together what might have happened. First, the splatters can show what weapon was used. For example, a blow from a baseball bat would cause blood to travel through the air with great force and speed. That would create one kind of splatter. The power of a gunshot might spray blood over a large area. That would create another kind of splatter.

Blood splatters provide other information, too. By following the trail of blood, police can often tell how the criminal and victim moved around the crime scene. Blood splatters can even show whether the criminal was right- or left-handed!

The Dingo and the Baby

"My God, my God, the dingo's got my baby!" Lindy Chamberlain said she screamed those words when she saw her two-month-old daughter Azaria being dragged off by one of Australia's wild dogs. Chamberlain, her husband Michael, and their three children had been camping with other families near Australia's Ayer's Rock. But that night—August 17, 1980—the trip turned into a nightmare.

Volunteers searched for the baby, but she was never found. A week later, though, a hiker discovered the baby's torn, bloody clothes. The clothes were carefully examined. Some experts felt that the stains and tears didn't match what a dingo's teeth and claw marks would do. There were also no traces of dingo saliva. Lindy and Michael were suddenly suspects.

An official court investigation, called an inquest, was held to determine what had happened. Eventually, it was decided that the child really had been killed by a dingo. Lindy's cool manner during the inquest, though, had turned many people against her.

LIndy Chamberlain and Azaria ➝

When: 1980
Where: Australia
Crime: Murder
Suspect: Lindy Chamberlain
Evidence: Blood

Traces of Blood

Despite the court's verdict, investigators continued to look for clues about what had happened. Eventually, blood was found on the front seat and carpet of the Chamberlains' car. Police also discovered blood on the blade and handle of a pair of scissors inside the vehicle. The blood was from a child less than six months old. Tests also showed that someone had tried to wipe the blood away.

Police now suspected that Chamberlain had slit her baby's throat in the front seat. Another inquest was held. "The first inquest was about dingoes," said one reporter, while "this one is about blood."

Prosecutors accused Lindy of Azaria's murder. A court at first convicted her. Many believed she was innocent, however, especially because there was some question about how the blood evidence had been collected. Finally, another piece of Azaria's clothing was found buried next to a dingo lair. Chamberlain's conviction was overturned in September 1988 and she was released from jail. In 1995, officials looked at the blood evidence one more time. This time, they returned an "open verdict." This meant officials could not determine how the baby died.

Wild dingo

GOING BUGGY

In 1235, a Chinese farm worker is found dead in a rice field. He has been killed by the long blade of a sickle. Village officials come to investigate.

The officials ask the farmhand's coworkers to place their **sickles** on the ground. Soon, flies swarm over one sickle. The insects are attracted by tiny bits of the victim's blood and skin still clinging to the blade. The owner of the sickle is arrested. Case closed.

Today, police still use bugs to crack tough cases. They rely on a forensic entomologist to provide the creepy, crawly evidence. An entomologist is a scientist who studies insects. By investigating which bugs are on, in, or near a body, an entomologist can estimate how long that person has been dead.

A Fly Went By

Perhaps no bug is as useful to the forensic entomologist as the common fly. Flies are the first bugs to arrive when a body starts to decompose.

Figuring out which species of flies are on a body is important. Different types of flies appear at different times and grow at different rates. Among the first to show up on a body are blowflies and flesh flies. The flies drink blood and other body fluids. Then the blowflies lay their eggs, usually in the body's mouth, ears, and other openings. Hours later, the **larvae** emerge from the eggs. The larvae are known as maggots.

Maggots such as these can help investigators pinpoint how many hours have passed since a victim's death.

The temperature of a decomposed body begins to rise as more larvae feast on the flesh. The longer a body decomposes, the more flies appear. So the number of flies and the heat of the body tell scientists a lot.

At some point the body begins to dry out. That leaves little food for the maggots. When that happens, other bugs, including rove beetles and hister beetles, arrive to feed. These bugs eat the remaining maggots and parts of the body where the flesh meets the ground.

Blowflies and flesh flies are among the first to show up on a body.

Body in the River

On June 23, 1989, two scuba divers came across a submerged car in the Muskegon River in Michigan. Inside the car was a woman's body. The medical examiner noticed that the woman had wounds on her head. The car crash did not cause these wounds, the medical examiner said. The woman had been murdered.

Police discovered that the car belonged to the woman's husband, David Smith. Smith told police that he and his wife had argued a few weeks before divers found the car. He had not heard from his wife since. Police were skeptical.

When: 1989
Where: Michigan
Crime: Murder
Suspect: David Smith
Evidence: Blackfly larvae

CASE CLOSED

When investigators searched the car, they came upon some clues— insects that spend part of their lives in the water. Police asked Richard Merritt, an entomologist at Michigan State University, to study the evidence. Merritt identified several types of insects: the caddisflies, the blackflies, and the midges. It was the blackfly that would crack the case.

The body of David Smith's wife was found submerged in a car in the Muskegon River.

Cocoons on a Car

The blackflies themselves were long since gone. But they had left their cocoons on the car. Merritt told police that blackflies spend the winter as larvae in the water. In the spring, they spin cocoons. They usually cement the cocoons to submerged rocks, or in this case, the fender of a car. Inside the cocoon, blackfly larvae develop into pupae, and then adults with wings. The insects emerge several weeks later, leaving the cocoons behind.

Merritt said if the car had gone into the river in June, as David Smith had said, the cocoons would not be on the car. Instead, Merritt said that the car did not go into the river later than April or May.

In 1990, the prosecutor convinced a jury that David Smith had clubbed his wife to death and dumped her body and the car into the river. David Smith was found guilty, thanks, in part, to the blackflies.

Developing blackflies live underwater.

Rick Merritt's knowledge of insects helped police piece together details of the crime.

WHO ARE YOU?

"Catch me if you can," Jack the Ripper teased in letters written to police and press. He had already committed several brutal murders in London, always targeting women. It was 1888.

Other than the bodies, police had little evidence to go on. They asked Dr. Thomas Bond for help. At that moment, Bond, a surgeon, became the world's first criminal profiler. Profilers are experts who try to determine the kind of person a criminal might be, and how he or she might think.

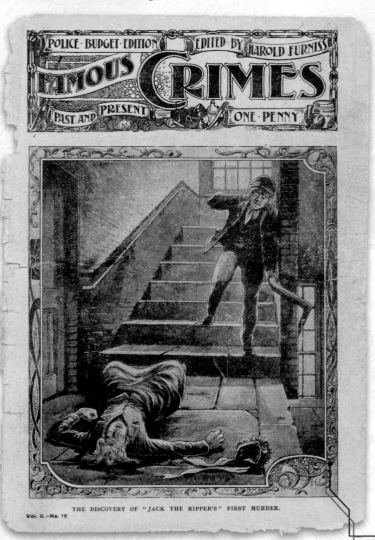

POLICE·BUDGET·EDITION EDITED BY HAROLD FURNISS

FAMOUS CRIMES

PAST AND PRESENT ONE·PENNY

THE DISCOVERY OF "JACK THE RIPPER'S" FIRST MURDER.

Vol. II.—No. 15

Bond looked over the evidence compiled by police. He also performed an autopsy on one of the victims, Mary Jane Kelly. Bond became convinced that one person committed all the murders. Despite the vicious nature of the attacks, Bond decided that the murderer probably appeared quiet and inoffensive, which caused his victims to trust him. Because of the way the victims had been mutilated, Bond suspected the murderer knew a lot about human anatomy. He probably also wore a cape, to hide all the blood.

Bond's conclusions seemed to make sense. Still, police never did catch Jack the Ripper.

Jack the Ripper became a favorite subject of "Penny Dreadfuls," cheap fiction publications that were popular in nineteenth-century England.

An Imperfect Science

Over time, police would add criminal profiling as a tool to solve crimes. Criminal profilers cannot tell exactly which person committed a crime. They can only make informed guesses about a type of person who might have done so. For example, a profiler might determine that a criminal has a certain job, or is well-educated, or lives alone.

Police generally call in a profiler when they are stumped. The goal is to narrow a field of potential suspects. Profilers use available evidence to try to figure out a criminal's personality and behavior. They read statements from witnesses and victims. They study police reports from the scene of the crime. They look at autopsy reports and study crime scene photos.

Despite what the movies and TV portray, criminal profilers do not have magical abilities, nor are they psychic. A good profiler will base a theory on evidence, not hunches.

Theodore Kaczynski, the Unabomber, set off sixteen bombs that killed three people. Before he was captured, he sent an anonymous "manifesto" to the *New York Times*. The ideas and language showed him to be well-educated and highly intelligent.

The Mad Bomber

It was 11 p.m. on a mild, foggy night in Waterbury, Connecticut, in 1957. Several uniformed officers quietly drove up to 17 Fourth Street, stopping in front of an old gray house with lace curtains. A few moments later, detectives walked up the steps and knocked on the door.

When: 1940s, 1950s
Where: New York City
Crime: Bombings
Suspect: George Metesky
Evidence: Letters to newspapers

George Metesky, a fifty-four-year-old man, opened the door and smiled. "I think I know why you fellows are here," Metesky said. "You think I'm the Mad Bomber."

Metesky was right. Police searched the house and found evidence of homemade bombs. Meanwhile, Metesky changed into a double-breasted suit and said good-bye to his two sisters.

Radio City Music Hall was one of the places George Metesky planted his bombs.

Educated and Insane

During the 1940s and 1950s, George Metesky made forty-seven bombs and set them off all over New York City. He planted them at Grand Central Station, the Empire State Building, and Radio City Music Hall. He sent local newspapers angry, well-written letters explaining his crimes. After several fruitless years searching for the Mad Bomber, police turned to Dr. James Brussel.

Brussel was a **psychologist**. He studied the letters and all the crime scene evidence and photos. He put together a profile of the bomber. Brussel said the evidence suggested that the bomber was a skilled mechanic who had once worked for a utility company. Brussel also concluded that the bomber thought he was smarter than most people, and probably lived with an unmarried sister or aunt. Almost everything Brussel said about the bomber proved true. But although police arrested Metesky, he did not stand trial. Instead, he spent nearly twenty years in a hospital for the criminally insane.

No Bones About It!

The skull was shattered, the bones in disarray. Could they belong to Josef Mengele, Adolf Hitler's "Angel of Death"?

Josef Mengele was a doctor who tortured men, women, and children with horrific medical experiments during the Holocaust of World War II. Because he was responsible for the deaths of so many, he was called the "Angel of Death." He later escaped and hid in South America. Years later, in 1985, searchers felt sure they had found his remains in a grave in Brazil. There was just one problem: the name on the tombstone was not his. So **forensic anthropologist** Clyde Snow was called on to determine whether it was Mengele in the grave.

Snow said the bones came from a right-handed white male between the ages of sixty and seventy. The height of the skeleton was almost a near-perfect match to Mengele. Next, Snow pieced together the skull and marked it with pins at thirty key points. He then took an old photo of Mengele and marked that with thirty pins. The pins on the skull and the pins on the photo matched perfectly. Snow had found the "Angel of Death."

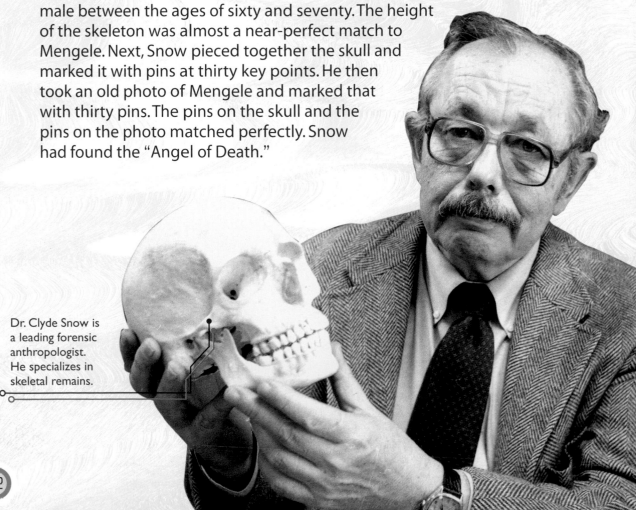

Dr. Clyde Snow is a leading forensic anthropologist. He specializes in skeletal remains.

Down to the Bone

Bones can tell a lot about a person. Bones can tell whether a person was male or female. They can also tell how he or she lived and died. For example, a slightly bent spine might suggest that the person was someone who carried heavy equipment for a living. Nicks in the bone might indicate the person was killed by a bullet or knife.

Scientists can also use skeletons to determine a person's age and race. Some forensic specialists can even take a skull and reconstruct what a person looked like by adding clay to a cast of the skeletal remains.

Forensic anthropologists often use teeth to identify a person. The width, spacing, and thickness of teeth vary with each person. Some people grind their teeth. Others have chipped teeth. Teeth also show signs of dental work.

TOOLS OF THE TRADE

Forensic anthropologists use the same tools and methods as archaeologists. Some of these tools are cutting edge. To find buried remains, for example, these scientists may use infrared photography and special metal detectors. They may even use radar that can penetrate the ground.

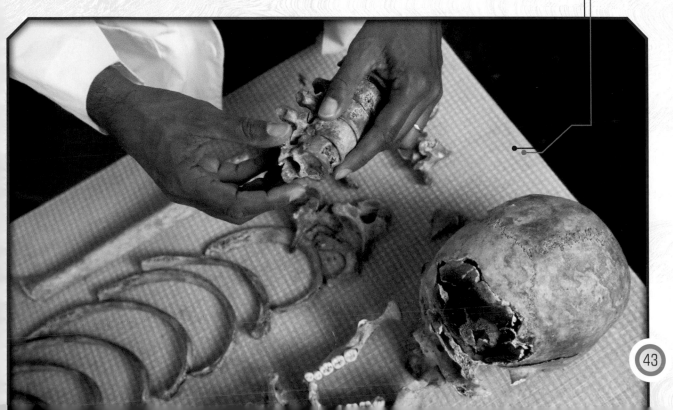

Bones of murder victims are laid out so that scientists can begin the identification process.

The Cannibal of Lake City, Colorado

Alfred G. (Alferd) Packer left Utah at the age of thirty-one with twenty others to mine gold and other minerals in Colorado. The prospectors arrived at an American Indian settlement in northwestern Colorado in January 1873. Members of the tribe told the men it was dangerous to travel beyond the camp in the dead of winter.

Packer and several others ignored the warning. They took a ten-day supply of food for the seventy-five-mile journey. The following April, only Packer emerged from the Colorado wilderness.

Police believed Packer had killed the others and eaten their flesh to get through the brutal winter. Packer was convicted of murdering the men with an ax just before eating them. He died in 1907, still claiming he was innocent.

In 1989, forensic anthropologists found the remains of the five prospectors. They determined that someone had hacked the men to death with an ax. No one knows for sure if the attacker was Packer—but someone killed those men.

When: 1873
Where: Colorado
Crime: Murder
Suspect: Alfred G. (Alferd) Packer
Evidence: Bones

↑ Alfred G. (Alferd) Packer boasted of his abilities as a wilderness guide, but he actually knew little about the wilderness.

THE FUTURE OF FORENSICS

What does the future hold for forensic science? Scientists are always looking for new ways to put criminals behind bars.

Extreme Technology

Researchers recently invented a portable wand that a CSI can use to find latent fingerprints in 10 to 30 seconds. Scientists are also working on a new technique that can tell whether fingerprints at a crime scene were left by a person who smokes. New technology can also link a digital photo to the person who took it by means of its pixels.

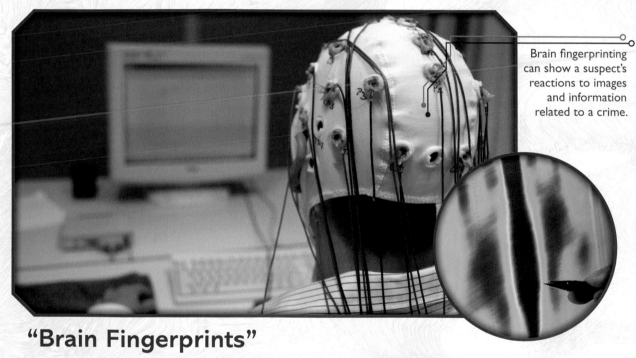

Brain fingerprinting can show a suspect's reactions to images and information related to a crime.

"Brain Fingerprints"

Even more amazing developments are on the way. For example, researchers are fine-tuning a device that, in essence, can read a criminal's mind.

Police hook up a suspect to a machine that records brain waves. Then, the suspect is shown a series of images related to the crime. As the suspect watches each image, a computer interprets the electric signals emitted by his or her brain.

"Brain fingerprinting" has a record of 100 percent accuracy in research with United States government agencies, actual criminal cases, and other applications. The results are admissible in criminal court cases.

GLOSSARY

anthropologist Scientist who studies the origin, behavior, and physical, social, and cultural development of humans.

autopsies Medical examinations of dead bodies, done to find the cause and time of death.

criminologist Scientist who studies crime, criminals, and criminal behavior.

decomposed Decayed; broken down into parts.

entomologist Scientist who studies insects.

fetus A developing human.

forensic anthropologist Scientist who studies human bones and skeletal structures.

isotopes One of at least two forms of a specific element.

larvae Newly hatched wingless creatures that have a different appearance from adults.

medical examiner Doctor who examines bodies and performs autopsies to determine the time and cause of death.

psychologist Person who studies the emotional and behavioral characteristics of an individual or group.

saliva A watery body fluid secreted by glands in the mouth.

sickle A sharp-edged semicircular tool used for cutting tall grass.

textiles Cloths and fabrics.

toxicologist Scientist who specializes in finding and examining drugs and poisonous substances in body fluids or tissue.

FIND OUT MORE

Books

Cooper, Chris. *Forensic Science*. New York: DK Children, 2008. Learn more about the techniques and tools investigators use to solve crimes.

Fridell, Ron. *Forensic Science*. Minneapolis, MN: Lerner Publications, 2009. Read how forensic science has changed from 1910 to the present and find out how real investigators have solved actual crimes.

Stefoff, Rebecca. *Famous Forensic Cases*. New York: Marshall Cavendish Benchmark, 2009. Learn the details of famous forensic cases through time.

Websites

www.centredessciencesdemontreal.com/autopsy/flash.htm
Investigate a murder with this cool flash game.

www.fbi.gov/kids/6th12th/investigates/investigates.htm
Follow a case from start to finish and learn how the experts solve crimes.

www.pbs.org/wgbh/nova/sheppard/analyze.html
Create a DNA fingerprint and solve a crime.

www.sciencenewsforkids.org/articles/20041215/Feature1.asp
This article provides good information on forensic science.

INDEX